Memory
Techniques
in a week

JONATHAN HANCOCK
CHERYL BUGGY

D0786085

Hodder & Stoughton

A MEMBER OF THE HODDER HEADLINE GROUP

Orders: please contact Bookpoint Ltd, 130 Milton Park, Abingdon, Oxon OX14 4SB. Telephone: (44) 01235 827720, Fax: (44) 01235 400454. Lines are open from 9.00 - 6.00, Monday to Saturday, with a 24 hour message answering service. Email address: orders@bookpoint.co.uk

British Library Cataloguing in Publication Data
A catalogue record for this title is available from The British Library

ISBN 0 340 84969 X

First published 1999
Impression number   10 9 8 7 6 5 4 3 2
Year   2007 2006 2005 2004 2003

Cover image: Photodisc/Getty Images

Typeset by SX Composing DTP, Rayleigh, Essex.
Printed in Great Britain for Hodder & Stoughton Educational, a division of Hodder Headline Plc, 338 Euston Road, London NW1 3BH by Cox & Wyman Ltd, Reading, Berkshire.

C O N T E N T S

Memory is everything. It drives every single thing you will ever think, say or do. And the way you feel about your memory is a big part of the sort of person you are and the quality of the life you lead.

At its best, memory connects you with the past, keeping alive people, places, experiences. Your memory helps you organise your work and the time in which you have to do it. It gives you access to vast amounts of information. It's stronger than the most powerful man-made computer, more versatile, more creative. It puts you in control of your world. But at its worst, memory is fallible and frustrating, inefficient and slow, prone to embarrassing lapses. It wastes you time, loses you money, puts everything into chaos.

Your memory is the most precious tool you have, but you need to know how to use it. Without proper training it will work well on some occasions and fail you totally on others. There will be things that you always remember, and things that you always forget, and you will be among the vast majority of people who feel that their memory is weak, and gradually getting weaker.

But learn how your memory works, start using it properly, and you will take your place in a privileged minority where memory is a priceless asset. However old you are, whatever job you do or stage of life you are at, you can quickly discover how to remember everything you need to know: names, faces, facts, numbers, lists, documents. You can start organising all the information that comes your way so that it is at your fingertips, whenever you need it, in a form that allows you to be efficient and creative. You can learn new skills, cope with change, improve your communication skills, your time-management, and more than anything, your confidence.

And when you understand how memory operates, you know how to make yourself memorable to others. People begin to remember the meetings you lead, the presentations you do, the instructions you give them. Your memory starts saving you time, making you money, and letting you enjoy a great feeling of control over your incredible, infinite brain.

This book includes everything you need to start putting your memory to immediate practical effect.

We will:

- highlight and then break down the barriers preventing you making the most of your memory
- explain how your brain's learning systems work
- outline tried and tested techniques for applying your memory to your particular needs
- take you through experiments and exercises that teach you the best memory habits
- help you develop your own long-term plan for enjoying your memory for life

Prepare to start getting the best out of your brain. There is nothing in your work, home or social life that cannot be done more successfully with a memory that is fit and active and under your confident control.

The right frame of mind

The Cray supercomputer weighs seven tonnes. Operating at 400 million calculations per second, it would have to run non-stop for a hundred years before it had achieved what your brain can do in a minute.

- You own more than ten billion brain cells
- Your brain can make more interconnections and create more new patterns of thought than there are atoms in the universe

The deeper we travel into external space, the more we know: but the further science takes us into the workings of the brain, the less we can say for certain. The brain's capacities are phenomenal, but its mechanisms are still largely a mystery. We race to think up new analogies for the way the brain seems to work, while struggling even to begin to comprehend its awesome potential.

Question – How much of the average brain's capacity will be used in a lifetime?

Answer – Less than five percent.

There has never been a time when memory power was so important, and so neglected. It is undeniable that the workplace is changing at a pace never before witnessed. All of us are inundated with new information: new names, techniques, procedures, rules, facts, ideas. Stress levels are high, the need to communicate quickly and to think creatively is greater than ever – and yet few people feel mentally equipped to deal with it all.

How often do you hear or, worse, find yourself uttering the following mantras:

- 'I've got a terrible memory'
- 'I can't cope with this new spreadsheet'
- 'I can't remember where I left that lap-top'
- 'Everything's just too chaotic...'

Stop. Within your head is more than enough brain power to cope with all the new data you face, all the changes you encounter in your working life. Your brain can deal with millions of pieces of information in the blink of an eye. You just have to use it properly.

Learn how your brain works, practise making it do what you want, and you can start tapping into its enormous potential.

The first step will always be to focus on the present – the way you try to think, learn and remember *now*. It's important to consider your current approach to learning, in order to highlight the bad habits and start focusing on the things that can be changed. Here's a learning task that you're unlikely to have to do in real life, but one that can help you to see the memory strategies you naturally employ.

> How would you go about memorizing the following number?
>
> 2821594434142463122635724

You have one minute to learn as much of the 25-digit sequence as you can. When the minute has passed, cover up the numbers and see how much of the order you can recall. This chapter ends with a technique for remembering the whole sequence with ease; but let's begin by considering what might currently be stopping you making the most of your brain's potential.

Negative mind-sets

You are the product of your experience. From childhood you have been on the receiving end of lessons, instructions, guidance and orders, from a number of sources. Parental influence led to that of teachers, your wider family, other adults, peer groups, and society at large. From that array of experiences, your view of yourself and the world has been formed.

The problem is, you almost certainly received far more negative messages than positive ones. Research suggests that, on average, ninety percent of the messages a child hears are critical or negative. It's hardly surprising then that many adults have deeply-rooted negative beliefs about themselves, and life in general. How often do you hear people say things like 'I'm not clever enough for that', 'I always failed in that in school', or 'I'm too long in the tooth to change' – and how often do you secretly agree with them?

Henry Ford said:

> 'Whether you believe you can do something, or believe you can't, you're right'.

One of the inevitable outcomes of a negative mind-set is that you're setting yourself up for failure even before you start. In many cases, you never even try something: fear of failure keeps you trapped in a familiar – but limiting – 'comfort zone'.

Yet we've all read about or spoken to people who are not limited by negative thoughts, not held back by fear of failure, not frightened to try something new. Focus on your negative ideas and challenge them.

For instance, if there's a nagging voice in the background telling you you're too old to start using your brain, you just have to look at the facts:

- ten billion brain cells
- ninety-five percent brain capacity unused
- a memory-bank already equivalent to an encyclopedia ten billion pages long

The latest research calls into question the assumption that memory automatically deteriorates with age. If you can use it properly and keep it in trim, your brain can do things you never thought possible – and *keep* doing them.

Habit

Humans are creatures of habit in what they do, and how they think. We like routine, doing things the way we've always done them – too often not the best way, just the way we've got used to. Generally we don't even realise that we're operating in a habitual way, cutting ourselves off from options that could dramatically improve our success.

Think of a habit you've broken in the past. A habit has to be learned, so it can be unlearned. It might have been tough, it might have taken a while, but remember the satisfying feeling of success when you achieved it.

To improve your mental performance, and to start learning
and remembering effectively, you need to identify the ways
of *thinking* that serve no useful purpose; thinking that
might be holding you back; thinking that you would like to
change.

As an example, imagine you'd decided to do something
about your habitual failure to remember people's names.
The process of change would be built on the following key
steps:

- *Accepting that your thought processes are simply
  habitual* – you've got into the habit of forgetting,
  and have no extra memory strategies to help you
  out
- *Stating to yourself that this particular habit serves
  no useful purpose* – even when you struggle and
  strain to remember, you still fail to recall key names
  at the crucial time
- *Acknowledge that you can change, because you
  want to* – a habit learned can be unlearned
- *Knowing that you can change, however old you are*
  – ingrained habits are harder to shift, but never
  impossible: remember the longer you've failed at
  something, the greater and more noticeable the
  benefits will be when you start to succeed
- *Seeing the advantages of change* – in this case,
  you would concentrate on the social and
  professional situations where remembering names
  is crucial: imagine the feeling of confidence you
  would have, and the sort of impact you could make
  on others

- Confirming to yourself that, from this moment on,
  you will actively work on remembering names,
  using the techniques you'll learn from this book.

Congratulations: you're on your way!

The way you've been taught in the past

When it comes to taking in new information, people have
different natural tendencies. Three key learning 'modalities'
have been identified:

1 **Visual** – seeing
2 **Auditory** – hearing
3 **Kinesthetic** – doing

Although we all rely on a mixture of the three, we tend to
dominate in one of the modalities.

Imagine you'd been given a barbecue kit to put together.
How would you go about it? Would you read the
instruction booklet? Would you ask someone to read the
instructions to you? Or would you feel happiest simply
playing around with the component pieces, exploring their
construction through trial and error?

Chances are you will plump for one and that is your
preferred modality. However there are those who use all
three to great effect. In doing so they are practising a form
of holistic learning.

It makes sense then, firstly, to know which is our preferred
modality so that in any learning situation we make sure we
receive information in that form.

Secondly, it's also a good idea to practise other modalities in order to flex the learning muscles and develop a more comprehensive approach to reinforce more thoroughly the information to be learnt.

By practising a multi-modality approach we can become progressive thinkers, and create a self-perpetuating circle of creative, challenging thoughts and positive feelings about ourselves.

Unfortunately, we can't always access information in the way we'd prefer. At school, it's estimated that children absorb as little of three percent of all the material they're presented with in lessons, because of this problem. So it's often experiences at school that lead to the belief that learning is difficult: it always felt so difficult in the past.

To recap:

You have at your disposal an enormously exciting mechanism for learning and remembering – your amazing brain. You may well be limiting your brainpower because of:

- a negative mind-set
- force of habit
- trying to use it in the wrong way

You need to commit to making use of some of that ninety-five percent of capacity that's currently standing idle.

So much for blockages to remembering and learning. What are the steps forward – the starting points for making this book work for you?

You need to be motivated

You won't succeed in anything if you can't see what's in it for you. Just as an athlete limbers up before an event, and focuses on the goal, before you begin your journey to effective memory you need to prepare yourself mentally.

What will you get out of improving your brain? Your list might include:

- dealing with information more quickly and more effectively
- saving time
- impressing others
- enjoying learning
- using new skills to boost promotion prospects
- increasing confidence

Spend a few minutes compiling your own motivating list, and make a point of looking back at it regularly.

You need a multi-faceted approach to learning

As touched on earlier, many people are turned off learning at school, and develop negative attitudes to their own abilities, because of the *way* they've been taught.

As young children, though, we don't have those problems. There was a time when we knew instinctively how to get it right. Think about the ways small children assimilate new information. They:

- engage all their senses
- give their imagination free rein
- ask lots of questions
- have little or no concept of failure
- remain enthusiastic and positive
- become totally engrossed in an activity
- try a variety of approaches

This is sometimes called 'global learning', since it involves the whole brain: the left, logical side, which deals with words and numbers, decisions and lists; and the right, random side, which attends to imagination, creativity, pictures and ideas.

As adults, we tend to limit our thinking processes, designating one thing as a problem requiring logic, and another as a challenge requiring imagination. The trick to effective memory and learning is to use both sides at once, and to benefit from all the options available.

You need the right learning environment

Today's workplace is often open-plan, busy, full of noise, movement and interruptions. It's fine if you can concentrate in that sort of environment – some people even prefer it – but it makes it difficult for those who need peace and quiet to think effectively. Just as we all prefer to take in information in different ways, we also have our own preferred places and conditions for learning.

Whenever possible, you need to take control of your learning environment. What sort of place would be ideal for you? Would it be:

- noisy or quiet?
- a small room or a large, open office?
- inside or out?
- heated or air-conditioned?

Experiment with the conditions, and be aware of all the tricks at your disposal for boosting focus and concentration.

- Tackle important information when you're most alert
- Let people know when you need private time and space to think
- Use a personal stereo, if a particular kind of music boosts your thinking power
- Surround yourself with visual images that please you, and be aware of how colours affect your mood
- Keep your workplace as organised and as calm as possible

You need to practise

All too often we abandon something without giving it a fair chance of working. We don't try as hard as we might to change an old habit and replace it with a new strategy, and reach for excuses to avoid practising it and putting in the work. 'I'm too busy', 'It's too difficult', 'Nothing's happening'. Suddenly the old, safe ways seem very appealing.

There's no magic wand or instant fix. Look back at your 'motivations' list – the things you could get out of having a powerful brain. Isn't it worth a little effort?

P.M.A. – Positive Mental Attitude

We've already highlighted the debilitating effect of the negative drip-feed many of us have been on. The following points will help you start to change negative into positive, and begin building the right attitude to learning.

Remember:

- change is possible
- the techniques for tapping into your true mental potential are simple to learn
- learning can be fun
- the benefits of a trained brain are immense

Stop:

- limiting yourself
- talking yourself down
- expecting failure

Start:

- trusting in your abilities
- seeing problems as challenges
- enjoying the rewards of your efforts

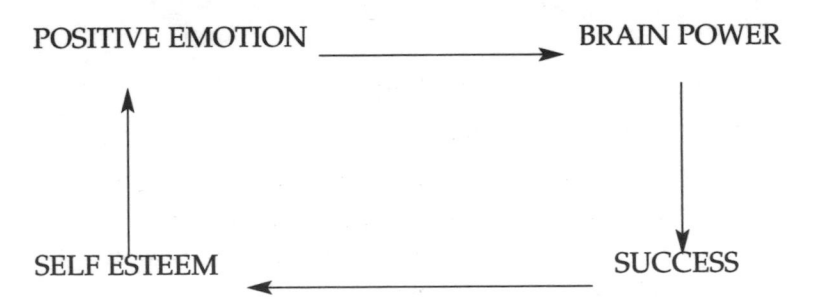

POSITIVE EMOTION ⟶ BRAIN POWER

SELF ESTEEM ⟵ SUCCESS

So, you need to ask yourself five key questions:

1 What's in this for me?
2 How do I learn best?

3 Where do I find learning easiest?
4 How can I start to practise?
5 How can I boost my beneficial thoughts?

Answer each of these questions in a positive way, and you take a dramatic step towards becoming a powerful and effective learner.

Learning habits may be deeply ingrained, but they can be changed – and when they are, the results are dramatic.

Near the start of this chapter you tried to learn a sequence of digits, using the approach that came naturally to you. Now, try learning it in a different way. It's possible to change information: to *make it memorable*. In this case, change the numbers into words. All you need is to remember the first two lines of a couple of very famous songs:

'I'm dreaming of a white Christmas,
Just like the ones I used to know'

and

'Should old acquaintance be forgot
And never brought to mind'.

Spend a few moments repeating the lyrics from memory, checking you can recall them accurately. If you can, then you now know the complete number sequence. Simply write down the number of letters in each word.

'I'm' has two letters, so you write down 2.

'Dreaming' has eight letters, so the next number in the sequence is 8. 'Of' has two letters, so next you write down 2 ... and so on. See how quickly you can write out the entire 25 digit number from memory.

This is clearly an artificial experiment, but it proves an important point. By adopting the right frame of mind, and showing a willingness to learn in a new way and to change information into a more memorable form, you can remember *anything*. It's even easier when you're motivated, and learning real information that's useful to you.

You've made a commitment to finding new and improved learning techniques – and now it's time to get to grips with how your memory works.

Your amazing brain

> *All knowledge is but remembrance.*
>
> *Plato*
>
> *If I had six hours to chop down a tree,*
>
> *I'd spend the first four hours sharpening the axe.*
>
> *Abraham Lincoln*

What's *your* approach to learning? Like Lincoln sharpening his axe, how do you prepare for a memory task, to make it as easy, enjoyable and efficient as possible?

Imagine you had to learn the following shopping list of ten simple items:

chocolates, potatoes, soap, milk, paper towels, coconut, bananas, cheese, wine, bread

Spend a few moments now trying to learn this list as you would normally. As you do so, make an effort to notice what you're doing. What habits have you picked up? How do you try to remember?

By the end of today, you'll be able to learn a list like this with ease, and recall the items forwards or backwards. In fact, you'll be capable of learning a list twice as long.

To learn how to do that, you need to understand how your memory works. We'll examine the physical mechanisms of the human brain, to get a glimpse of how this amazing resource works, and how it must be fuelled and operated.

First, though, we need to ask a fundamental question: *Why* does it work? Why does the memory work sometimes – but not always?

Almost everyone claims to have a terrible memory, but they don't seem to think that it's *always* terrible. In fact, they're in no doubt that it works very well for them sometimes.

A man who forgets his wife's birthday every year may be a doctor with a mental database crammed with hundreds of thousands of medical facts. A woman who says that she can't remember telephone numbers could easily be a keen musician, and know countless pieces of music off by heart.

One of the most important steps in memory improvement is simply realising that some things are easier to remember than others. Our brains do work, and we prove our own memory power many times every day – but not every type of information sticks easily. Like Lincoln and his axe, you need to invest time preparing for the task, altering information to make it memorable.

We do this already. Everyone at some time will have made use of mnemonic tricks. 'Thirty days hath September...'; 'Every Good Boy Deserves Favour'; 'Richard Of York Gave Battle In Vain'. Perhaps you remember certain numbers by spotting patterns, noticing significant digits – your age, for example, or your house number. Unfortunately, few people ever get to know about the really powerful memory techniques – the ones that let you change *any* kind of information to make it compatible with the way your mind works.

To discover what they are, you need to test your memory. Use the following experiment to find out the characteristsics a piece of information needs to have, if it's going to be memorable. Read through this list of 25 words once or, if possible, get someone to read them out to you. As soon as the list is finished, see how many of the words you can write down from memory, in any order.

> shoe, watch, flower, Madonna, chair, lion, kettle, ball,
> pin, firework, pencil, tiger, phone, warm, puma, hill,
> time, sharpener, mugger, cheetah, hat, car, apple,
> book, kite

What's most interesting about this test isn't how many words you remember – but which ones. It's possible to predict with surprising accuracy which words most people recall.

book, kite – you're likely to have remembered the last two words on the list because there was very little time to forget them. No new words appeared to confuse you, so you were able to carry them in your short term memory for long enough to write them down.

shoe, watch, flower – the words from the very start of the list are also likely to have stayed with you. When the experiment began, your mind was fresh and alert. You were interested in the sort of words that might be included, and it's likely that you were making a special effort to remember.

On the other hand, the words from the middle of the list are a great deal harder to recall. Your interest wanes, your mental energy drops, your concentration wavers and the whole task just seems too difficult and confusing.

lion, tiger, puma, cheetah – most people who try this test spot the four linked words – the big cats – and remember them all as a group. Perhaps you found that this also worked for *pencil* and *sharpener* – two words that you could easily link together in your mind.

Madonna – when a words stands out from a set of information, is noticeable and unusual, it's much easier to remember.

firework – being able to picture a word is a vital part of remembering it. In this case, the word also conjures up sounds and even smells, making it particularly powerful, especially compared to the abstract words in the list like *warm* and *time*.

mugger – this word is likely to have provoked an emotional response, making it much more memorable than bland words like *pin, phone* and *hill*.

From this simple test, key factors about memory are revealed.

You remember:

- when your mind is alert, you're interested and motivated, especially at the start and end of any learning period
- when material is patterned or connected
- when information is unusual
- when you can picture what you have to learn
- when the information makes you feel something

You forget:

- when you lose interest and motivation, especially in the middle of a learning period
- when the material has no shape or connections
- when information is dull
- when it's difficult to picture the material
- when what you're learning doesn't provoke any emotional response

If you consider these points in terms of your day to day memory experiences, you'll see that they make sense.

The sort of information you tend to remember is:

- material you're interested in, or really motivated to learn, like statistics about your favourite sport, or material to help you make money
- songs, tunes and poems – connected into memorable patterns of sound and rhythm
- stories, also based on connections, with one event causing another, one scene linking on to the next
- faces – you know you've seen a person before

- unusual events – the days when you did something out of the ordinary
- embarrassing moments, times of happiness, fear, surprise – all occasions made memorable by strong emotions

Of course, most information we have to learn doesn't conform to these points. We waste so much time struggling to remember things that – as they're presented – simply aren't memorable:

- numbers – abstract, hard to visualize or connect
- names – you recognize the face, but what's the name? Again, the name is abstract, easily confused and forgotten
- everyday jobs – you don't feel particulaly motivated, the information is dull and uninspiring, and so you regularly forget it

So the best kept secret of memory is this: if information is difficult to learn, you need to change it, to make it memorable.

Making it memorable

It may well be a step that you've never really considered before, but it will revolutionize your learning. Learn something well enough the first time, and that's it – you don't have to re-learn it endlessly. Information is made compatible with the way your memory works, and so learning it is easy and efficient, saving you time in the long run and boosting your confidence and success. Well-learnt information is there whenever you need it, wherever you are – and in a form in which it can be explored, organised and then produced in the most effective way.

So how do you make *any* kind of information memorable?

There's a one word answer to that: **IMAGINATION**.

The Emperor Napoleon once said that 'imagination rules the world'. We all have powerful imaginations, seen in dreams and fantasies, and used when we're reading books, listening to radio plays and working through problems. It's imagination that allows us to take information and change it, to make it memorable. As long as you can return it to its original form when the time comes, it simply makes sense to explore and learn it in a form that your mind can handle.

It's time for a little imagination training. Below are four everyday words. Spend a few moments picturing each one in your imagination. In the first instance, simply try to imagine each object with as much clarity and in as much detail as possible.

- box
- tree
- car
- cake

Next, return to each item, and imagine picturing it from different angles. Can you imagine walking round it, seeing it from above, even getting inside it and looking out.

Now try adding some sense information. Imagine touching the item: what does it feel like? Is there any smell, sound or taste? Add as many details as you can to your imaginary pictures.

Next, practise making information unusual. Anything is possible in the imagination, so make each of your four images as unusual as possible. You could visualize the objects in a strange place, or doing odd things, or becoming very large or incredibly small. Exaggerate to make the images bizarre and memorable. These skills are vital when it comes to powerful learning and remembering. You take control of information in your imagination, make it visual and unusual, and give yourself a range of sense triggers.

Feelings are also important. To practise the skill of inventing emotional reactions to information, go back to the first word, *box*. You should already have a memorable image in your mind – but your task now is to imagine *destroying* it. How would you go about wrecking the box?

What would your feelings be like as you ripped it up, set fire to it or attacked it with a chain saw?

Next, imagine you're scared of the *tree*. How could you use your imagination to make this tree the most frightening thing in the world?

Turn the *car* into a source of hysterical fun. How could you picture it so that it made you roar with laughter?

Finally, invent an embarrassing moment involving the *cake*. Involve yourself in the action, and imagine the feeling of utter embarrassment.

Visual

Unusual

3-dimensional

Stimulating to the senses

Stimulating to the emotions

As soon as a piece of information has been given these characteristics it can be connected with others in a memorable pattern. It's like inventing a story about your material. Each item becomes one step in the story, prompting you to remember the next.

One item can transform into another, or explode and release the next image. You can imagine joining items together, putting one thing on top of another, or seeing something come to life and do something bizarre and memorable to the next item on the list. Remember, anything is possible in imagination. The story doesn't have to have any real logic – only the connections you create.

To link these four words together in a story, you might imagine opening the box to find a tiny tree inside. You could take the tree and fix it to the rear view mirror in your car, and then drive off – straight into a giant cream cake sitting in the middle of the road.

- Think of the *box*, and you'll remember finding the *tree*
- Think of the tree, and you'll recall fixing it in your *car*
- Picture driving off in your car, and you'll remember how you felt when you smashed into the giant *cake*

BOX ⟶ TREE ⟶ CAR ⟶ CAKE

However long a list is, you only need to deal with one item at a time. Make each link strong enough, and it'll take you to the end of your story.

The structure of the brain

To help you appreciate just what your brain is capable of; let's take a look at how it is structured.

Saint Augustine said 'People travel to wonder at the highest of mountains, at the huge waves of the sea, at the long courses of rivers, at the vast compass of the ocean, at the circular motion of the stars and they pass by themselves without wondering'.

Inside our heads we are wondrous indeed. In fact, the more we explore our amazing inner universe with all its range and its complexities, the more we realise there is to discover.

There are three clearly defined areas of the brain.

1   *The Reptile brain.* Also know as the stem brain, it oversees the primitive survival mechanisms such as self-protection, reproduction, nourishment and shelter. It is also responsible for understanding physical reality, collected via the senses.

2   *The Mammalian brain.* This brain area represents a quantum leap in terms of evolutionary development. It is here that feelings, emotions, memories and experiences are assimilated. It is also the part of the brain that deals with bodily needs and functions such as hunger, thirst, sexual desire, body temperature, metabolism and immunity. Having collected a vast array of information via the senses and bodily sensations, it then passes that knowledge on to the largest part of the brain, the thinking part.

3   *The Cortex.* This part makes up around eighty percent of the total brain. Here resides the intellect, where reasoning, decision making and linguistic ability results in purposeful voluntary actions. It is here too that many believe the sixth sense of intuition can be found. This is the part of us that is able to perceive information that is not picked up by our other senses. It is the superior qualities of the cortex that stand us apart from all other living things and make us unique as a species.

As well as this tripartite brain there is another division into the left and right hemispheres. These are responsible for the different modes of thinking, and they specialise in particular skills.

The left hemisphere. This works in a logical, rational, linear and sequential manner. It takes responsibility for such things as speech, writing, details, facts and organisation.

The right hemisphere. This part of the brain works in a disorganised, random but more holistic way. It relies on intuition, and deals with feelings, emotions, visualisation and aspects of creativity. Although each part of the brain has its own particular responsibilities, all the parts communicate and interact with each other. If we delve at a more microscopic level into how the brain works, it becomes even more fascinating.

We have literally millions of neurones. These brain cells, each unique and with special responsibilities, pass messages back and forth throughout the brain to the central nervous system. They are able to do this via electrical and chemical reactions. Under the microscope a neurone could be mistaken for a minute creature from the deep. It consists of a central body with feathery tentacles known as dendrites. The dendrites have attachments called synapses, where the exchange of chemical signals takes place. Once stimulated by a chemical signal, a dendrite sends an electrical impulse to the cell body. This triggers a larger electrical pulse onto the axon, which acts like a lightening conductor. It channels the signal at great speed through its length, and out to other cells in the brain. An outer coating of the fatty protein myelin, helps enhance the speed at which the message travels. The final stage of the process occurs at the synapse, the junction between one neurone and another.

Neurones store information and act together to cause actions and reactions. They work in assemblies, each with specific tasks. Some deal with the outside world through the senses and movement, while others are responsible for internal communication between the areas of the brain to ensure we can think, imagine, create and be aware. These assemblies communicate with each other and with other assemblies, simultaneously sending and receiving messages over great distances and at phenomenal speed, while also being aware of the whole needs of the body. Truly formidable.

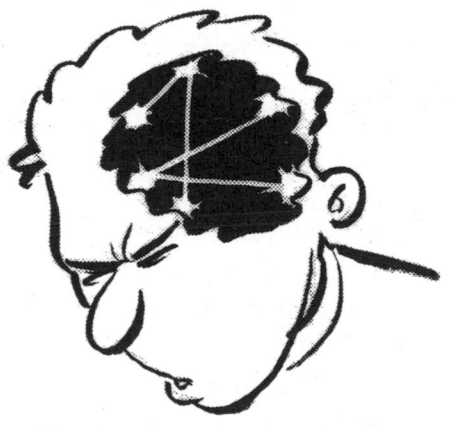

The latest research indicates we possess around ten billion neurones in the cortex alone. Each neurone can have as many as 20,000 synapses on its dendrites, which roughly adds up to one million billion possible connections with other neurones. Add to that the fact that each cell can react or fire up around five hundred times a second, and it's clear that the human brain is breathtaking, and its capabilities awesome.

Where memory fits in

Memory itself is also complex, and most scientists now
accept that memory is stored in different parts of the brain.
There are also different types of memory.

Procedural memory. This is the unconscious ability to do
such automatic things as run, drive a car, ride a bicycle,
play a piano or juggle.

Semantic memory. This is where our knowledge of the world
is stored. For example it is your semantic memory that
knows that kangaroos come from Australia and that
Sydney has an amazingly designed opera house.

Episodic memory. This is the memory that records and stores
past events, but is not always reliable. For example your
semantic memory might record facts about Australia, but
you might not be able to remember all the details of a
holiday you spent there.

Prospective memory. This is the system that lists the things
you have to do in the future. It is one of the most unreliable
of our memory systems.

In terms of our brain's development, much will have
depended on our childhood experiences.

Generally speaking the raw material for full brain
development is in all of us at birth. If that raw material is
nurtured we will mentally blossom. For that to happen we
need comprehensive physical and emotional support, and
effective models that provide example and stimulus. The
more meaningful your teaching and learning has been, the
more effectively and thoroughly are the connections made

between neurones. It is then easier to make reconnections and new connections.

The good news is that whatever your childhood experiences and whatever your age is now, you can effectively activate your brain and tap in to your remaining brain cells. That means taking advantage of the ninety–five per cent still left to use!

Storytelling

Let's return to the list of words at the start of this chapter.

> Chocolates, potatoes, soap, milk, paper, towels, coconut, bananas, cheese, wine, bread

Here's an example of how an imaginary story could be created to turn each item into a memorable picture, and then to link each one to the next.

ACTION

Imagine...

...opening a box of expensive chocolates, only to discover to
your horror that each one has been replaced with a potato!
You investigate further by starting to peel one of the
potatoes, and you discover when you bite into it that it's
made out of soap. You need to get the taste out of your
mouth, so you take a long drink of milk, but unfortunately
the carton has a leak, and the milk pours all over you, and
out across the floor. More and more milk is pouring out,
and you try to mop it up with some paper towels, but it's
no good. The level is rising fast. Sitting on top of the towel
rail is a coconut. As you watch it grows and grows, until
it's big enough for you to sit on and float on top of the
milk.

A banana floats by, and you fix it on to your coconut boat
as a mast – then use a large triangular piece of cheese as a
sail. You find a bottle of red wine on board, and use that to
paint a colourful design on your sail. Unfortunately you've
been a bit rough, though, and a number of holes have been
torn in the sail – which you try to patch up with pieces of
bread.

Read the story through again, trying to picture it all vividly.
After that, see how many of the ten shopping list items you
can remember. Simply go back through the story in your
mind, link by link, and write down each item as it appears.

It began with a box of chocolates. Inside that were potatoes,
which turned out to be made of soap. You tried to get rid of
the terrible taste with milk, but the carton leaked and you
used paper towels to mop it up – in vain. As the milk levels
rose, you used the huge coconut as a boat, and fitted it with
a banana mast and a cheese sail. You painted the sail with

wine, tearing it in the process – and the story ended with you repairing the holes with pieces of bread.

It might help to imagine filming the strange events. Your mind's eye becomes a camera, able to zoom in on key details, move with the action, and explore everything that's going on. When you replay the mental film, you'll be able to recreate all the details of the story.

Put the technique into practice. Lay aside any other strategies or habits you might have picked up. Most important of all, be positive. Don't be tempted to think that the following list is too long to learn. You're only dealing with one item at a time, so it could be *any* length, and you'd still be able to remember it.

Bear in mind all the key points. As you go along, each item needs to be visualized, made unusual and memorable, and then connected vividly to the next. Abandon all normal logic, but make sure there's a strong reason for you to remember the next item on the list – and the stranger, more exciting, frightening, embarrassing, violent or funny the link is, the better. Exaggerate, and let your imagination run riot.

Here's the list: 20 everyday words. Take as much time as you need to transform the list into a memorable story, then play it back in your mind's eye and see how many of the words you can write down, in order. There's no reason why you can't even do the same thing in reverse. Simply follow the chain of events back to the start.

television, clown, rabbit, fire, tea, pocket, scissors, snake, bin, castle, slide, bush, money, newspaper, ant, sandwich, ring, basin, coal, cat

Think like a genius

Global thinkers

Many of history's most famous thinkers and achievers have a single trait in common – the ability to use all of their brain.

Thumbing through a book that explores the sketches of the artist Leonardo da Vinci, one is struck by his breadth of subject matter and inventiveness. He was not only a highly gifted artist, he was also an engineer and military expert, possessing a degree of curiosity, ingenuity and universality of mind that made him outstanding. Lewis Carroll made his living teaching mathematics at Oxford University, but he also tapped into the abundant creativity of his imagination when he wrote Alice's Adventures in Wonderland and Through the Looking Glass. Albert Einstein – still one of the figureheads in the world of science – also explored the world of philosophy. He once said 'Imagination is more important than knowledge. It is a preview of life's coming attractions.'

What these exceptional men had in common was an approach to knowledge that is described as *global*. As outlined in yesterday's chapter, as well as the brain being divided into three parts, reptile, mammalian and cortex, it is also divided into two sides, left and right. The left side is responsible for logical, rational, linear and sequential thought, while the right side looks after the more intuitive, holistic, random side of our thinking.

da Vinci, Carroll and Einstein did not just tap into one side of their brain, they capitalised on both. Although specialists in their fields, they had such curiousity and vision that they made use of both the left and right sides – and thus they widened the scope of their expertise, whether it was to paint sublime pictures and design flying machines, or work on the intricacies of mathematics while writing about a young girl walking through a mirror into another reality.

Although we all do tap into both sides of our brains, we tend to prefer to use one side or the other. We shy away from pushing out of our comfort zones to explore and practise ways of thinking we consider difficult. We're leaving so much brain power untapped.

A global approach means that the brain is being utilised fully. Learning becomes easier, more can be achieved, thresholds and limitations challenged. The saying, 'None of us is as good as all of us', could well be applied to how we approach using our brain's capabilities. What we need to do is to develop our right-brained modes of thinking, such as feelings, emotions, music, creativity and visualisation, as well as the left-brained modes of verbal and written communication, organisational and rational abilities – and, crucially, start putting the two sides to work *together*.

Global learning is further enhanced by using the senses and by immersing oneself in a subject. By diving in and becoming engrossed and asking the who? what? why? when? how? questions, understanding is enhanced and learning becomes even more effective.

The added advantage of adopting the global approach is that it also produces positive emotions via increased brain power, and encourages us to be even more adventurous in our thinking.

More memory practice

Don't worry that you'll get confused between the different mental pictures you create and stories that you invent. Your memory is unbelievably powerful, and able to keep all the different batches of information separate.

Put this principle to the test by learning another list of words, and then checking that you can still remember the 20 words you learned at the end of the last chapter.

Here's the new list of words:

grass, elephant, computer, matchbox, mirror, football, rocket, biscuit, caravan, fence, spade, cow, tent, cloud, lamp, shorts, basket, train, sun, glass

Remember the key characteristics of memorable information. These words need to be visualized in as much colour and detail as possible, exaggerated and given sense and emotion triggers, then linked together into an unusual, connected story. Give yourself a maximum of ten minutes to commit this list to memory – to *make it memorable*. As soon as you've completed your story and checked that you can remember all 20 words, return to the first list, and read out *those* twenty words – beginning with *television*.

You now have 40 items committed to memory, in two distinct mental 'files'. As long as each story is built on strong links, they won't overlap or become confused. In each case, the first word is all you should need to start off the chain of images – and you'll find that you can recall the list backwards as well as forwards.

> Memory techniques like these may seem disordered and fanciful, but in fact they create a real sense of organisation and precision.

Picture clues

So far we've worked with lists of objects, each of which provided a definite image. This means that you can memorize lists of shopping or presents, or all the items to be taken on holiday, but what about information that's harder to visualize? What happens when you need to remember words that suggest no obvious pictures?

The trick is to use *picture clues*. You think up a picture to remind you of your original information. It may well be very different from the actual word you're trying to learn, but it'll be enough to jog your memory. Picture clues can be based on how a word sounds, what it looks like, or on an image that it suggests. You can use any picture that works for you.

As an example, imagine you had to learn the following list:

First ten U.S. Presidents since the Second World War

Truman, Eisenhower, Kennedy, Johnson, Nixon, Ford, Carter, Reagan, Bush, Clinton

Here are some suggestions for picture clues but the best ones are always those that you think up yourself.

- *Truman*: perhaps a cricketer, like *Freddie* Truman, or someone taking a lie-detector test to prove that they're a 'true man'.
- *Eisenhower*: maybe you simply think of 'ice' – or it could be an 'ice shower'.
- *Kennedy*: you could picture Barbie's boyfriend Ken, or maybe a rocket being launched from the Kennedy Space Centre.
- *Johnson*: the image here could be of Johnson's baby powder, or the actor *Don* Johnson.
- *Nixon*: perhaps a Nikon camera, or a thief 'nicking' something.
- *Ford*: a river-crossing or a Ford car.
- *Carter*: a man pulling a cart.
- *Reagan*: a ray gun.
- *Bush*: a bush.
- *Clinton*: Clint Eastwood perhaps.

Spend a few moments coming up with an image clue that works for you, for each of the ten presidents' names. Once you have your images, learning them is as easy as learning the items on a shopping list. Simply take each one in turn, connect it with the next, and build up a memorable story.

You might imagine...

...Freddie TRUMAN, still wearing his cricket gear, climbing into an icecold shower – EISENHOWER – only to find Barbie's plastic boyfriend Ken – KENNEDY – in there already. Ken is covering himself with Johnson's baby-powder – JOHNSON – before he poses for photographs taken using a top-of-the-range Nikon camera – NIXON. The photographer races off to get the pictures developed in his FORD car, but he's driving so fast that he crashes into a CARTER. Enraged, the carter pulls out a ray gun – REAGAN – and the poor photographer tries to hide in a nearby BUSH but Clint Eastwood – CLINTON – is already using it to hide from the Indians...

Whatever kind of story you create, run though it a few times in your mind, checking that you can remember all ten picture clues and that each one links clearly to the next. When you're confident with your imaginary tale, use it to write down the names of the ten presidents from memory.

Check that you can still remember the two lists of twenty words – one began with *television*, the other with the word *grass* – and the ten item shopping list. All the pieces of information should be there in their individual files: already that's 60 pieces of data memorized with ease.

Image illustrations

With practice, you'll get used to thinking of a picture to represent any kind of information. Often you don't need to worry about every last bit of the original material – just think of a picture that's going to jog your memory. After all, without these techniques you'd probably remember the information *eventually*. It's in there *somewhere* – you just need a prompt to retrieve it when you really need it.

Say you wanted to learn the following list of jobs to do in a day at work:

1. Set a date for the office party
2. Order new calendars
3. Buy a present for Paul
4. Arrange a game of squash
5. Pay cheques in to the bank
6. Book your holiday

You might come up with the following image 'illustrations' for each job:

1. The party itself, full of sounds, tastes and feelings
2. A large, colourful calendar
3. Paul, holding his present
4. A squash racket
5. Large cheques
6. A sun-baked beach

You could then connect the images into a story like this:

The office party is in full swing, and the noise is so great that all the calendars fall off the walls. One hits Paul as he's opening his present and he collapses, unconscious. You

prod him with your squash racket to check he's OK, then
write him a cheque for compensation, which he uses to pay
for a holiday in the Caribbean.

If you ran through that chain of images a few times on your
journey to work, you'd have a powerful memory story to
help you organise your day. You could consult this mental
checklist wherever you were, and make sure that all the
key tasks were completed by the end of the day.

Numbers

So far we've concentrated on remembering words and
phrases, but it's also possible to use the same basic
techniques to memorize numbers.

These days, most of us don't need to remember large
amounts of numerical information. What we need to get to
grips with are PIN codes, burglar-alarm settings, addresses,
extension numbers, birthdays, times – all mostly made up
of just a few digits. Having a strategy for learning these
small groups of numbers saves a great deal of time and
trouble.

As with the lists you've learned so far, the trick is to think
in pictures. You need to invest a little time deciding on a
picture to represent each of the ten digits, 0–9, so that you
always have an image-clue to use.

On a blank piece of paper, jot down the ten digits, with
enough space alongside each one to write a brief
description – or make a quick sketch – of the image you
give it.

You could base your images on what a digit looks like. In that case, you might draw a ball next to 0, or write 'sun' or 'orange'. Next to the number one you could write 'pen' or 'pencil', or draw a needle or pin. You just need to think of one key image for each digit.

You might base some of your images on what a digit sounds like, choosing something that rhymes with it. Two could be 'shoe', three might become 'bee', four 'door' and so on.

Another possibility would be to make use of the significance a digit might already have. If you were born on the sixth day of the month, for example, you might illustrate six as a birthday present, or write 'birthday cake' on your piece of paper. Seven could become one of the Magnificent Seven, eight an After Eight mint.

When you've come up with an image for each of the digits, check that no two are so alike that you'll get confused. You can also fine-tune your system as you use it, so don't be afraid to develop and improve your set of ten images.

Using this number system is simple. To learn a group of numbers, you just transform each digit into the image you've assigned it, then connect the images together into a scene or story. The one crucial extra step is to make the scene appropriate to your reason for learning the numbers in the first place.

For example, if the code to disarm your burglar alarm was 3264, then your number system might give you these four images:

BEE SHOE BIRTHDAY PRESENT DOOR

You could imagine a huge honey-bee landing on your shoe. You try to squash it with a birthday present, but the bee flies off and out of the house through the open front door.

BEE on SHOE, threatened with BIRTHDAY PRESENT flying through DOOR – this simple scene gives you the four important numbers: 3264.

The final step would be to connect this scene with your reason for learning the four numbers. You might imagine sounding the alarm as the bee escapes – to remind you that these images give you the code for the alarm.

Perhaps you want to remember that the PIN code on your bank card is 7205.

For seven you might have an image of HEAVEN (rhyme).

Two might be represented by a SWAN (shape).

Zero could be a FOOTBALL (shape).

Five might turn into a HOOK (shape).

You might picture yourself standing in heaven, when you see a majestic swan. You climb onto its back, and enjoy flying – until you realise that people on the ground below are pelting you with footballs. To get your own back, you burst every one you can catch, using a large metal hook.

To connect this strange tale with the original numbers, you might imagine seeing an animated version of it on the screen of a familiar cash machine. Every time you use a machine for real, you'll remember the cartoon – and see yourself in HEAVEN, climbing onto the SWAN, being pelted with FOOTBALLS and bursting lots of them on a HOOK: your bank card PIN must be 7205.

Practise using your own number system by memorizing the following historical dates.

> *Remember*
> * Step One: Turn each digit into the appropriate image
> * Step Two: Connect the images into a short story
> * Step Three: Connect the story with your *reason* for remembering.

Dates:
Gunpowder Plot: 1605
Death of Ovid: 17
Battle of Waterloo: 1815
Henry the Eighth born: 1491
Ruin of Pompeii: 79

Below are five UK dialling codes. See how quickly you can use your system to commit them to memory – and remember you don't need to worry about the first two digits each time, because all STD codes begin with 01.

Dialling-Codes:
Newcastle: 0191
Liverpool: 0151
Oxford: 01865
Peterborugh: 01753
Birmingham: 0121

Any kind of information can be given a picture clue, and those pictures linked into memorable stories. The information is simply being made compatible with the way human memory works.

How to remember anything

One of the best things about the sort of learning described in this book is that it cuts out wasted repetition. Once you've created pictures and stories to remind you of a set of information, you never have to start again from scratch. You can quickly recap the material even if you haven't used it for months, simply by reminding yourself of the key images – and every time you do so you're strengthening the memories, rather than just learning the same material again.

Spend a few minutes now recapping some of the information you've learned so far in this book, the images and stories that allow you to recall:

- the ten item shopping list, beginning with CHOCOLATE
- the list of twenty words beginning with TELEVISION
- the list of twenty words beginning with GRASS
- the first ten U.S. Presidents since World War Two
- the dates of
  - the Gunpowder Plot
  - the death of Ovid
  - the Battle of Waterloo
  - the ruin of Pompeii
  - the birth of Henry the Eighth
- the dialling code for:
  - Newcastle
  - Liverpool
  - Oxford
  - Peterborough
  - Birmingham

You're able to remember any kind of information by *making* it memorable, and so far you've learned more than seventy distinct pieces of information.

Practice makes perfect – so try memorizing the first ten numbers in Japanese. Don't be tempted to think that this is too difficult. The technique is one you're well used to by now. You simply invent an image-reminder for the way each number sounds, then link all ten together.

1 ichi	6 roku
2 nee	7 nana
3 san	8 hachi
4 she	9 q
5 go	10 ju

Image ideas:

1 and 2 – itchy knee
3 – sand
4 – sheep
5 – 'go' sign
6 – rock
7 – bananas
8 – a sneeze (it sounds like 'hatchoo!')
9 – a queue
10 – juice

Perhaps you imagine yourself...

...rubbing your itchy knee in the sand, when a flock of sheep rush at you, knocking you flying across the beach. You try to get rid of the sheep by holding up a large sign saying 'Go', but it's no good: they're all settling down for the day on rocks by the shore, and opening up their picnic boxes – which are all full of bananas. Unfortunately, sheep must be allergic to bananas because they all start sneezing – 'hachi!' – and form a long queue at a stall selling juice, which they hope will wash away the offending taste.

itchy knee... san(d)... shee(p)... go... rock(u)...
(ba)nana... hachi... q(ueue)... ju(ice)

Ten images, each jogging your memory about a Japanese number.

The best images and stories are always the ones that you think up yourself, so spend a few minutes putting your imagination to work on this list. Check it through a few times, reinforce or change difficult or confusing parts – then test yourself by covering up the list and reading all the numbers back from memory. If you were to recap your story a few times every day, within a week you'd know this list by heart.

The best kept secret

Stories are powerful tools for giving otherwise abstract and unconnected pieces of information a memorable structure. But there is another strategy – one that has been called 'the best kept secret' about your memory. It makes learning faster and easier, it works in the way your brain likes to work, and it has been used with incredible success for centuries.

Ancient Greek legend has it that super-rich Scopas threw a huge banquet, during which disaster struck. His banqueting hall collapsed on his hundreds of guests – among them Simonides, the poet, one of a handful of survivors. Identifying the bodies would have been impossible, had it not been for Simonides' trained memory. By closing his eyes and mentally rebuilding the banqueting hall, he was able to connect every guest with their location in the room, and provide a perfect guest list and seating plan from memory.

Simonides lived at a time when memory systems were taught and celebrated. How else could one teach, speak, argue cases of law or compose epic poetry without a practised ability to do it from memory? By Roman times, using mnemonic strategies came as second nature to great orators such as Cicero, who is known to have addressed the senate for days on end from memory. Before they were taught what to remember, students were taught how to remember it – and the central element of every memory system was what has come to be known as the 'Roman Room' concept, or the 'Memory Palace'. Simonides used the framework of a banqueting hall to contain the information he needed to remember the guests, and you too can use the frameworks – buildings, golf courses, towns, walks – of your everyday life to store vast amounts of information in an incredibly useable way.

It is a natural tendancy of the human brain to think spatially, and to connect abstract information with concrete places. Have you ever got to the top of the stairs and forgotten what you were coming up for? If you return to the spot where you were standing when you had the urge to go up, your memory may well kick back into action. Detectives often take eye witnesses back to the scene of a crime to help them remember exactly what they saw. If you listen to music as you drive around, it is likely you can recall where you were the last time a particular song or piece of music came on. The Roman Room technique capitalizes on this strong link between memory and location. It makes use of the fact that you already know from memory many hundreds of mental frameworks into which information can be slotted and stored.

The Route System

Step 1. Pick a building you know well. This technique also works well when you use walks, car journies – even golf courses – but it's easiest to start with a simple building: your home, where you work or perhaps a hotel you visit regularly.

Step 2. Divide this building into ten separate areas. It often helps to sketch out a quick plan on a piece of paper. The areas could be rooms, particular features or whole floors – just however you think the building can best be divided into ten zones.

Step 3. Decide on a route, from area one to area ten. It's important that you're sure of the route, because you'll always take the same mental walk around this building. What would be the most logical way of getting from the first area to the last?

Step 4. Close your eyes and imagine moving along the route. Start by picturing yourself standing in area one. What can you see? What does this place smell like and sound like, and what details set it apart?

From there, visualise yourself moving to area two. Again,

bring this zone to life in your mind's eye. Keep doing this, going from place to place and spending a few moments in each one, until you arrive at the end of your route.

Step 5. As a final check, see if you can imagine making the journey in reverse. This shouldn't be a problem: in real life you have no difficulty remembering the way out of your house or back home from work. It's just a good way of making sure that you're fully confident with this memory route.

When you've completed these five steps, you're ready to put your route to use. It's been time well spent: you'll be able to use this mental structure many times, to help you remember many different types of information.

To use a route, you simply locate a different piece of imagery in each of the ten areas. These are exactly the same sort of image clues used to remember words, names, ideas or numbers. The route system just removes the need for a story to link them together: instead, the connecting structure is already decided upon. All you have to do is slot in the images.

Use your imagination to fix each image in place as powerfully as possible. As you make the mental journey around this building, think of unusual, funny, violent, memorable ways of placing an image into each room.

As an example, here's a sample route around a typical house:

1. front porch
2. hallway
3. living-room

4. dining-room
5. kitchen
6. sun room
7. staircase
8. bathroom
9. bedroom
10. study

If you were using this route to memorize a shopping list – apples, coffee, cakes, butter, sugar, oranges, mineral water, salt, treacle, cereal – you could imagine...

...stepping into the front porch, and finding a huge APPLE filling the room. You have to squeeze around it to get into the hallway, which is flooded with hot COFFEE. Imagine the smell, and the feeling of the hot liquid as you paddle out into the living-room. Here, all the furniture is made out of CAKE: a cake sofa, cake dresser – even a cake TV. You walk into the dining-room, where a meal has been set out on the table – but the only thing on every single plate is a block of BUTTER – hardly a balanced meal! In the kitchen, every cupboard, tin and pan is full of SUGAR. Imagine opening up a high cupboard, and being showered with an avalanche of sugar.

The next area on this route is the sun room. Here, ORANGE-trees are flourishing in the warm sunshine – and the whole room is painted bright orange. The staircase has been turned into a cascading waterfall – but a very expensive one, using gallons of MINERAL WATER. There are three rooms upstairs. In the bathroom, the bath is full to the brim with salt. Imagine what it would feel like to take a bath here – and how it would taste if you accidentally got a mouthful! Lying down in the bedroom is just as uncomfortable, because someone has spilled sticky TREACLE all over the bed clothes. Your journey ends in the study, where the books on the huge bookcase have been removed – and replaced with packets of CEREAL. There's cereal all over the carpet, and the desk – it's even got into the expensive computer.

In practice, filling up a route like this is extremely fast. Once you've done it a few times, you'll be able to imagine moving from room to room with ease, and take just a few seconds to visualise fixing each image in place. Try it, and you'll find that retrieving the imagery is almost unbelievably easy.

In the example route, you'd instantly remember:

- the apple blocking up the porch
- the coffee flooding the hallway
- the cake furniture decorating the living-room

- the butter served up in the dining-room
- the sugar filling the kitchen
- the oranges growing in the sun room
- the mineral water cascading down the staircase
- the salt filling the bath
- the treacle spilled in the bedroom
- the cereal all around the study

Design a route of your own. Follow steps 1 to 5, then put your framework to use straight away to learn the following list of items to pack for an imaginary holiday.

> sunglasses, suncream, swimming costume, passport, travellers' cheques, camera, sandals, maps, tennis racket, toothbrush

It's useful to have several routes organised in your mind, so that you can use them in rotation. Once used, you'll find that the imagery has disappeared from each route by the time you come to use it again. On the other hand, you can fill a route with information of lasting value to you, recap it every so often, and retain it as a permanent resource.

Take time now to design a second route. Make it memorable, different from the first, but follow the same five steps. When you're confident of this second mental structure, practise using it by committing the following information to memory:

Bodies of the Solar System, in order from the sun

1. Sun
2. Mercury
3. Venus

4. Earth
5. Mars
6. Jupiter
7. Saturn
8. Uranus
9. Neptune
10. Pluto

As with the list of U.S. Presidents and the Japanese numbers, you first need to come up with an image-clue for each of these heavenly bodies. Here are some suggestions, but feel free to think up your own:

1. Sun – your son, or the Sun newspaper
2. Mercury – a thermometer
3. Venus – goddess of love
4. Earth – a pile of muddy earth
5. Mars – a Mars bar
6. Jupiter – perhaps a duplicator, or a 'dew pit'
7. Saturn – Satan
8. Uranus – uranium
9. Neptune – sea god
10. Pluto – Mickey Mouse's dog

Once you've got your ten image clues, you simply fix them into place around your route. Always be on the lookout for appropriate ways of slotting them into place, and try to make use of things already present in your mental structure – items of furniture, for example, as 'hooks' to hang them on.

If your second route was based on your workplace, for example, you might imagine pages from the Sun newspaper pasted across the window of your office; a thermometer fixed to the control panel in the lift; a pile of earth in the middle of the boardroom table etc.

Give yourself enough time to fix each of the ten images in place, then see how quickly you can write them all down, in order, from memory. If you have trouble recalling any of them, simply leave a space and go on to the next area. It may take a little time to recall a few stubborn images, but all the clues are there somewhere.

When you're confident with this new data, spend a few minutes recapping the other information you've learned:

- the ten-item shopping-list, beginning with *chocolates*
- the list of twenty words, beginning with *television*
- the list of twenty words, beginning with *grass*
- the first ten U.S. Presidents since World War Two
- the dates of:
  - the Gunpowder Plot
  - the death of Ovid
  - the Battle of Waterloo
  - the ruin of Pompeii
  - the birth of Henry the Eighth
- the dialling codes for:
  - Newcastle
  - Liverpool
  - Oxford
  - Peterborough
  - Birmingham
- the first ten numbers in Japanese
- the ten items to take on holiday
- the ten items on the shopping list beginning with *apples*

Along with the Solar System list, that's 110 separate pieces of information, neatly arranged in mental files. Every time you recall them like this, you fix them even more firmly in your mind.

One of the most powerful benefits of the routes system is that whole sets of information can be fixed into each mental space. This means that you could easily create a single route to hold details of all the projects you were working on, or all the jobs you wanted to get done in a given week, month or year. The route system gives you the power to be highly organised – but, within that framework, to be creative too, adding and removing images whenever necessary.

Memorizing sets of information

Using the 'house' route described earlier, here's an example of how *sets* of information can be included and memorized.

You might decide to make the front porch your 'staff training' room, if that was a key part of your work. You could decorate it with picture clues to remind you of:

- the outdoor activity course you need to book (rope swings and balance beams fitted around the porch)
- the names Judy and Roy, staff members you need to see about their appraisals (Judy might be performing a Punch and Judy show in a cupboard, and Roy could be sitting on the window-sill dressed as Rob Roy)
- the date 1st July, an important deadline (the digits to remember are 1 and 7, and this might give you the images PAINTBRUSH and HEAVEN – so you could imagine using the paintbrush to create a dramatic illustration of heaven on the front door)

Whenever you return to the front porch in your mind, you'll find it filled with image clues for all the key details to remember about staff training. You can add new pictures when necessary, and remove those that are no longer required. To do that, either visualize the old images being removed or rubbed out, or simply stop highlighting them in your mind, and let them slip away naturally from your memory.

You might decide to make the bathroom your area for remembering details about the key tasks you need to accomplish before the end of the month. You could imagine:

- finding the bath full of old door signs (since you need to order new ones)
- flushing computer disks down the toilet (to remind you to replace a key software product)
- discovering Ben Hur using the shower to wash his golf clubs (to make sure you remember to organise a game of golf with your colleague Ben)
- seeing Ben Hur use his shoe to kick oranges around the bathroom (giving you the digits 2 (SHOE) and 0 (ORANGE), and thus a reminder to arrange the match for the 20th)

The mental routes you create can also help you read, digest and remember texts and documents. As you read, get used to breaking the information down into key points. You're going to be illustrating each point with an image clue – so what *are* the key points? How much detailed information do you need to retain, and what images would jog your memory about each main point?

As you're reading, jot down key words or phrases that would act as a sufficient 'crib sheet'. Reading a memo about a change of premises, for example, you might jot down:

- moving
- 5th December
- Derby
- 3 new jobs
- Paul in charge of project

When you'd finished, you would give each point an image clue. Perhaps you imagine choosing slides to illustrate this information in a visual presentation. What picture would be appropriate for each idea?

You might choose:

- a removal van
- someone using a hook (5) to pull a nail (1) out of a shoe (2) – 5/12
- a Demolition *Derby*
- worker *bees* (3)
- the dome of St. *Paul's* Cathedral

Fixing the images into one of your memory routes, you might imagine:

- a removal van crashing into the porch
- a cobbler at work in the hallway, using his hook to prise a nail from a shoe
- a Demolition Derby taking place in the living-room
- three worker bees eating at the dining-room table
- the kitchen transformed into St. Paul's Cathedral

As always, the process written down looks more complicated than it is in practice. You could easily slot images into your route as you read through the text, and the habit of thinking in pictures is an easy one to pick up. Soon you'll be condensing all the material you read automatically, and coming up with memorable illustrations with ease.

Reading like this is almost certainly slower than you're used to but how often have you 'read' a whole page without taking in a single piece of information? *Active* reading is much more focused, so it feels more tiring to begin with, but you do it in shorter bursts – and get out exactly what you put in. Give it a try, and soon you'll be reading not just for the sake of reading, but to understand and learn.

A recent newspaper article analyzed a report about the things people liked least about their working life – and how they would go about making changes if they could. It broke the 'moans' and 'wishes' into two lists of ten key points – just as you could have done if you were presented with the entire research document.

To practise illustrating ideas picked out of larger texts, and fixing the images into a route, try coming up with a picture to represent each of the ten 'wishes' printed below, then arranging them around one of your mental frameworks.

Top Ten Wishes
1. to work shorter hours
2. to change 'company culture'
3. to work flexible hours
4. to avoid commuting
5. to work from home
6. to change job
7. to have more staff
8. to earn more
9. to retire
10. to have less stress

Learning to learn

You have a test approaching, your emotions are in a turmoil as you realise you have just so much to remember. Your mind appears blank as you spin into panic. There is an important presentation looming, you feel stressed and anxious, convinced you will forget everything and make a fool of yourself. The radio interview which will give you the opportunity to talk about your company and its work is tomorrow, but how will you remember your name, let alone get your message across? Such responses are typical: we've all felt that sinking feeling. Somehow it seems that whatever it was we did know has been lost in the recesses of our brain.

However it doesn't have to be that way. If you begin to put the following advice into practice and do the necessary preparation, you are putting yourself in the best possible setting to meet with success. It's good to know that by regularly using these tips and techniques you can enhance your ability to learn, remember with ease, get those answers right, interview with high impact and make a memorable presentation without reading from copious notes.

Step one: put yourself in the best learning environment for you. There is little point struggling to learn effectively if where you are working is too noisy, too quiet, too hot or too cold, too untidy or too bare and unwelcoming. Whatever is best for you, try to create it before you start to tackle whatever it is you have to learn and remember. It is worth mentioning that current research concludes that the colour of the room you are in, the music you might be playing, the smells you are inhaling, the pictures on the walls, even how you are sitting, can all have a profound impact on your emotions and therefore your attitude to your work.

Step two: ensure you are in a positive frame of mind. Feeling good about yourself and your abilities and anticipating a good outcome to your endeavours is very important. Just as no athlete worth his salt would dream of approaching the starting blocks of a race with a negative mind set, so you should see a successful outcome to your work. Recognise negative self talk and replace it with something more constructive and positive.

You might find using creative visualisation techniques could help you here. This is a method of relaxing and mentally creating a positive outcome to whatever it is you are about to embark on. It is a way of setting yourself up for success not failure.

Other techniques include using affirmations. This is a method of repeating positive statements about yourself and your abilities. There is also the reframing technique. Here you choose to banish negative self talk and select the positive way of viewing something.

Remember everything has a positive aspect to it if you really look hard enough. Choose to view your abilities and your approach to learning in a new way.

Step three: see what's in it for you.
Now that may be easier said than done especially if you have to deal with information that does not exactly excite you. But whatever you're tackling, you're much more likely to remember it if you can see what use it will be to you and how it will help you. In this way you become an *active*, not a *passive*, learner. Remember, there is a positive gain in everything, if you are prepared to look for it.

Step four: be prepared to re-learn.
We are creatures of habit in the way we think, and
consequently we can limit ourselves by the mental
boundaries we have set ourselves as a result of past
experiences. Reframing, thinking outside the box, accepting
there might be other ways of approaching a subject, and
seeing the big picture, all help to encourage a more
proactive stance to learning and retaining information.
Remember too the importance of the global approach to
learning that we covered in the previous chapter.

*Step five: be courageous and don't be defeated by past mistakes or
learning problems that seem insurmountable.*
It could be the case that the way you were taught in the
past did not suit you, but you can do something about that
now by knowing and using the learning style that is right
for you, be it visual, auditory, kinesthetic, or a mixture of
all three. It's all too easy to stay in one's comfort zone
rather than going out and trying new ways of learning and
new areas of knowledge. Don't limit yourself or subscribe
to the 'Better the devil you know' mentality.

*Step six: be clear about what you want to achieve from what you
are about to learn.*
At the same time realise how much you already do know in
order to boost your confidence. Be willing to look back at
past successes and victories to see how far you have come
already. Why not make a list of what you have achieved so
far? Keep a note book that celebrates your successes, on the
walls stick up pictures, photographs, certificates, anything
that is a constant reminder of good positive experiences. Do
not subscribe to the negative statement that self-praise is
not good for you.

Step seven: reward yourself regularly for what you are achieving.
If you have been working hard and meeting the targets you
have set yourself, what's wrong with taking a day off to do
something you really enjoy, or treating yourself in the
shops? It's also important to nurture yourself if the going
gets tough. Be kind to yourself. A day at a health spa, a
relaxing aromatherapy bath, laying in a hammock with a
glass of wine and a good book might be ideas you would
like to consider.

Step eight: keep yourself in tip-top condition by eating well,
sleeping well and taking regular exercise.
A balanced healthy eating programme not only helps
prevent unnecessary wear and tear on your body, it also
energises you and helps you keep mentally fit. Getting
enough good quality sleep should also figure in helping
you operate at your optimum level. If you are not sleeping
well consider how you can relax and let go before going to
bed.

Do you need to invest in a new mattress? Would using essential oils on your pillow help? or playing relaxing music? or using ear plugs? Also try to ensure you are taking regular exercise, at least twice a week. Sometimes just getting up a little earlier for a brisk walk can help set you up for a more energetic positive day, and certainly after a day full of pressure, exercise helps burn off excess stress.

Step nine: crucially, practise by going over the knowledge you are acquiring and have acquired.
Ensure you put the information you need into your brain in a meaningful way, then revisit it regularly to further reinforce it.

By using these tips and techniques you will find that you are building a strong and healthy mental attitude to learning and remembering. Your outlook will be positive as you approach new information. Also your ability to absorb facts more comprehensively and with greater ease, means you will have far more confidence when it comes to recalling information for any tests, or approaching interviews, presentations or communications of any kind.

So how can you begin to take action to ensure you incorporate this advice into your everyday life so that you are in the best possible frame of mind to learn and remember?

Action

1. Are you in the best learning environment?
   What changes can you make?

2. Do you have a positive mental attitude?
   What improvements can you make?

Action

3. How can you get the most out of any learning experience?
   What's in it for you?

4. What mental barriers have you set up? Name a limitation around learning or memory that you have imposed on yourself?
   Where has it come from?
   How can you change it?

5. What is your preferred learning style? How could you improve your abilities in the other modalities?
   Mentally revisit a mistake or failure. How can you now regard it in a more positive way?

6. List five recent successes in order to appreciate your abilities.
   List five more you want to achieve.

7. How can you reward yourself when you do well?
   How can you pamper yourself?
   How can you nurture yourself when the going gets tough?

8. How can you improve your diet?
   How can you improve your exercise regime?
   Are you getting good quality sleep?
   Are you taking time for relaxation?

Action

9. How can you practise what you are
currently absorbing about memory
and learning?

To conclude today, let's see how well you have
remembered the lists from the previous days.

What are:

- the ten item shopping-list, beginning with *chocolates*
- the list of twenty words, beginning with *television*
- the list of twenty words, beginning with *grass*
- the first ten U.S. Presidents since World War Two
- the dates of:
  - the Gunpowder Plot
  - the death of Ovid
  - the Battle of Waterloo
  - the ruin of Pompeii
  - the birth of Henry the Eighth
- the dialling codes for:
  - Newcastle
  - Liverpool
  - Oxford
  - Peterborough
  - Birmingham
- the first ten numbers in Japanese
- the ten items to take on holiday
- the ten items on the shopping list, beginning with *apples*
- the top ten 'wishes'.

People skills

One of the traditional party-pieces of the stage memory performer is remembering the names of every member of the audience. American magician and mnemonist Harry Lorayne made it his trademark, reciting theatrefuls of names night after night. One estimate put the number of names he had successfully recalled at eight million.

Many great military leaders, politicians and businesspeople have demonstrated equally breathtaking abilities to remember names. And yet for most people, remembering even one new name at a time is too much.

Perhaps you know what this feels like: you are at a conference, talking to a colleague, when a recent acquaintance comes over to join them and it's up to you to introduce them to each other – and suddenly you cannot remember either of their names. But imagine the opposite effect. Think how powerful it would be to be able to put names to faces at meetings and parties; how effective to remember key facts about the people you do business with; and how useful to know enough about memory to make everyone you meet remember you.

Step One is to listen, to hear people's names when you are introduced to them. Slow the process down: practise asking people to repeat their name if you missed it. Give yourself time to take it in.

Step Two is to be interested in every new name you hear. Ask where it comes from, what it means, how it's spelled.

Step Three is to switch on your mind's eye and visualize the name. Spend a couple of seconds imagining what the name would look like written down, or how it might come out as a signature.

Step Four is to think of picture clues. What images come into your head when you think of the name? You're only looking for image triggers, so you might pick just part of the name to turn into a picture – an object, place or animal. Perhaps you think of a well-known person who shares the name, or a friend or relative of yours. You are making a vital memory move – moving away from abstract names to images that are real, unusual, interesting, colourful and memorable.

As the pictures start to emerge, Step Five is to try to make some connection with the real person in front of you. Imagine them holding whatever image has occurred to you, standing in the place that came to mind, or turning into the famous person you thought of. Think of their name as *illustrating* them in some way, and use your imagination to connect them with the image clues their name suggests.

For example, if you meet John Butcher, his name might well suggest meat, knives, chopping boards, roast dinners. As you talk to him, picture him taking out a huge meat cleaver and chopping great hunks of meat. As always you can involve your senses, switching on every facet of your memory, fixing your new friend in your mind with some powerful memory joggers.

With practice you can carry out these five steps quickly, without them getting in the way of conversation, and learn to give yourself enough memory clues to negotiate a meeting or party. Afterwards, it is up to you how many of the new names you choose to remember permanently. You can invest time in rehearsing the most important names and adding extra details so that you remember them long into the future.

Here are some more examples of image clues:

Surnames

- Anderson: perhaps someone hiding in an Anderson air-raid shelter, wearing a gas-mask
- Shelley: covered in sea-shells
- Rowling: constantly performing forward rolls
- Jones: singing in the style of Tom Jones
- Cathcart: pulling a cart piled with cats

First names

- Leo: lion
- Kate: kite
- Mark: covered in dirty marks
- Mike: holding a microphone
- Donna: prima donna ballerina

Leo Shelley could be visualized roaring like a lion *and* covered with shells. Mike Rowling could be trying to talk into his microphone *and* do hundreds of forward rolls. The trick is to build up a set of images, using all the time at your disposal to add extra reminders.

Every new piece of information can also be given an image and added to the mental scene. You might picture Kate Jones flying a kite while singing Tom Jones songs – at the same time as working out on an exercise bike and reading a book – representing the two hobbies she's told you about. If you recalled an image of Donna Anderson dancing around her air-raid shelter – and talking to a man in a fig-leaf – you'd remember that her husband was called Adam.

Remember people's names a few times by using these techniques, and you'll soon find that you know them off by heart. The strange imagery fades away, and you'll have forgotten *why* you know them – you just *do*.

Don't worry about getting names wrong. There are plenty of jokes about people confusing mental images and making embarrassing gaffes, but in reality this rarely happens. Mnemonic techniques just give you extra chances for learning more names – and when you get in the habit of remembering, that feeling of confidence is often enough in itself to make you remember.

Printed below are ten names, along with an extra fact about each one. Learn them all by using one of your mental routes. Think up images to jog your memory about each first name, surname and personal fact, then fix them in the spaces around the route.

> Tom Bird: enjoys fishing
> Sheila Walker: comes from India
> Richard Welsh: works with computers
> Arnold Donald: has a wife called Jean
> Tracey Cole: keen tennis player
> Jane Webster: American
> Ronald Smith: enjoys cooking
> Tara Singh: accountant
> Shaun MacDuff: keen horse-rider
> Juan Domingo: married to Maria

To recover the information, simply retrace your steps, moving from room to room in your mind. Each area on the route should contain clues to three key pieces of information: first name, surname, and personal detail.

When you're confident with the imagery you've created, see how much of this information you can write down from memory. You may not remember every single person you meet, but these techniques will certainly help you feel more confident about keeping track of the important ones.

Thinking creatively like this is also a good basis for creative conversations. If you get used to thinking in pictures from the first moment you meet someone, then you're in the perfect frame of mind to discuss ideas and possibilities, and to solve problems. You'll also be aware of what it takes for other people to remember *you*. Give them time to hear your name and take it in. When you're talking about yourself, try to speak in pictures and stories, suggesting images and emotional responses for them to latch on to.

It can only benefit you if people remember you, and even simple strategies like these can be more effective than the most expensive business card.

Communicating effectively from memory

Talks, interviews and presentations
What you have already learned about how the brain functions, and how we learn and remember best, can stand you in good stead when it comes to performing in the public arena. You can tailor-make your message to appeal to all of your audience by considering the following nine points.

1. Ensure you paint pictures with the words you use. Remember how the brain likes unusual, dramatic exciting images. Make use of similes and metaphors.

2. Tap into the three modalities by giving your audience something to see, hear and do.

3. Include such information, and present it in such a way, that it will appeal to both left- and right-brained thinkers. Make use of the power of tapping into the senses of your listeners. Is it possible or appropriate to appeal to their sense of sight, feel, taste, smell and touch?

4. Put yourself in the shoes of your audience. Carry out some research. How do they think? Create empathy by understanding that people are mentally moved first by the way they habitually think, then by their feelings and emotions. Help them to make connections with things they already know in order to lead them into new territories, and if possible personalise the messages you are sending them. Tap into what will move or influence them emotionally.

5. Know that the way you open and close your presentation is important in terms of the powerful images you create. People pay most attention at the beginning and end of an interview or presentation, so it is also crucial to ensure your audience don't lose interest in the middle of what you are saying. Pay special attention to how you structure that part. Again make use of images, paint pictures, tell a story, give your listeners something to see, hear and do. Make links and connections with what has already been said and signpost where you are taking them next.

6. Before you begin any presentation or interview, anticipate success by visualising how it will be. See yourself being well prepared, dynamic and interesting and being well received by your audience. See and feel how receptive and appreciative your audience is. Experience how great you'll feel as you pat yourself on the back! Now practise and rehearse to perfect your performance. Imagining is powerful but certainly not enough on its own.

7. Using the learning and memory techniques you have been introduced to in this book, you can now create your whole presentation mentally by organizing the key

information in one of your chosen routes. Take memory joggers by all means, but just think how impressive it will be to give your performance without once losing eye contact with your audience or fiddling with pages of notes. We are always impressed with those who show they know their subject so thoroughly that they speak without a script.

8. If you are going to use visual aids, remember to make them colourful and meaningful to give them impact. Use images and few words. Don't forget, 'a picture paints a thousand words'!

9. Remember the importance of positive self talk. Cultivating a positive mental attitude not only transforms the way you feel about yourself, it also gives a new and powerful dimension to the way you appear to others. You find you are full of energy and conviction, qualities that make your audience sit up and listen. Don't forget you are your best visual image!

So what action can you now take to improve the impact you will have when you next give a talk, interview or presentation?

Checklist.

1. How can you improve the language you use?
2. How can you tap into the three modalities?
3. How can you appeal to left- and right-brained thinkers?
4. How can you engage the senses of your listeners?
5. How can you empathise with their points of view, their needs and their emotions?
6. How can you open and close powerfully?
7. How can you keep them interested in the middle?
8. Can you visualise success?
9. Can you select the key points of your presentation interview or talk and place those points in one of your mental routes or settings?
10. How can you improve your visual aids?
11. Finally what positive messages can you send yourself about your abilities and skills as a presenter or interviewee?

The importance of lifelong learning and a personal improvement plan for your memory

Becoming a lifelong learner.

The term 'lifelong learning' seems to be on everybody's lips these days. However, it is something that has always been practised by high achievers and those who have become great and inspiring role models over the centuries. Such people have naturally high curiosity and great enthusiasm for knowledge. They automatically keep their minds stimulated, challenged and exercised, as we saw earlier with the likes of da Vinci, Carroll and Einstein.

You may not feel that you wish to emulate those who have reached such dizzy heights of achievement, but by reading and taking part in the exercises over the past week, perhaps you now realise just how much potential you have inside your head. Your brain is waiting, willing and very able to help you learn and remember. As it is bursting with potential, why not choose to tap into it and stimulate some of the spare millions of brain cells!

The good news is, the very fact that you have bought and read this book puts you in the category of lifelong learning already. To continue the process, here are some suggestions.

See the advantages
As a result of committing to lifelong learning you are likely to:

- Continue to build and maintain high self esteem
- Stretch your mental muscles
- Push out of your comfort zone and explore exciting new realms of knowledge
- Develop new skills
- Keep fresh, stimulated and motivated
- Create and sustain a positive learning energy cycle
- Improve your knowledge
- Improve your earning potential
- Become more creative
- Use more of your brain
- Feel more excited by life and all it has to offer

How to do it
How can you ensure that lifelong learning becomes part of your everyday existence?

- Create the space to learn. Make use of travelling or waiting time and use books or audio tapes to gain new knowledge. Get up a little earlier than usual and combine jogging with a walkman or an exercise bike with a book!

Read in the bath and in bed. Turn the television off more often.

- Sign up for some classes, or another professional qualification. There is so much on offer these days. Such courses offer structure, aid purpose and direction, and sharing learning aids stimulus.
- Identify the need. What could you learn that will give added benefit to the work you do or the quality of your life?
- Is your learning environment as beneficial as it could be? Could you create a space where you know you will be in the best possible atmosphere to learn? Don't forget, even on a crowded train you can make use of a walkman. Remember too that you will have a preferred time of day for learning, and that the short intense burst approach might be better for you than taking huge chunks of time for studying.
- Try to immerse yourself in your chosen subject or subjects. Be wide and deep in your approach. Be aware of how much you already do know.
- Check out your health. Do you need to make changes in your diet? Are you fit? Do you need a routine medical check? Are you sleeping well?
- Are you using your preferred learning style? Make sure you are absorbing new information in the way that is most beneficial to you. At the same time, try to build your strengths in the other modalities to enhance the global approach. Consider your brain as an exercise gym. The more you use the different apparatus on offer in a gym, the fitter your whole body becomes.
- Also try to use both sides of your brain to capitalise on left- and right-brained learning. Challenge yourself. If, for

example, you consider yourself to be poor at mathematics, challenge that assumption. Realise that it is a negative thinking habit holding you in that frame of mind, and start some maths classes, or buy some books to help you improve. Think what that will do to your confidence, as well as developing more of the left side of your brain.

- Keep hold of a positive mental attitude and don't put yourself down when you make mistakes. Be enthusiastic and excited by knowledge. An outlook like this will simply grow and blossom.

Tips for retrieving stubborn memories

Work has been done to highlight strategies for improving the recall of eyewitnesses to crimes – and it reveals tips for retrieving stubborn memories. There are four key points.

1 Recreate the initial conditions
Witnesses to crimes or accidents are often asked to try to
remember exactly what the weather was like. How warm
did the air feel? Was it windy? They also try to bring back
their own feelings. Were they hungry or thirsty, sad or
happy, excited or bored, on the day the incident occurred?

This is also useful when you're trying to recall imagery
from a memory story or route. Try to tap into general
memories, and to recall feelings, and you may well recover
the precise images you're looking for.

2 Concentrate on details, no matter how unimportant they seem
We've seen that the brain works on a pattern of
interconnections, and that information needs to be
patterned and connected to suit it. It follows then that any
details you remember can be used as a starting point, to
begin a chain of associations back to the detail you're trying
to recall.

If, for example, you return to an area on one of your mental
routes and remember a detail that seems unimportant to
the main image you're looking for, it's still worth
concentrating on it and seeing what it yields. It could
suggest something else; that might link to another thought
– and suddenly the key image appears.

3 Visualize a remembered scene from another point-of-view
Witnesses to bank robberies might be asked to imagine
what the *robbers* must have seen – and you can use the
same principle to boost your recall. Get used to visualizing
a mental route, story or scene from different angles, and
letting your mind's eye search out the detail you're
missing.

4   Replay a memory in reverse

After road accidents, eye-witnesses are sometimes asked to replay the events backwards: visualise the crashed cars ... then describe what happened just before the crash ... and what led to *that* ...

It's a particularly useful strategy when you're trying to remember by using a story or route. If it doesn't work perfectly one way, try recalling it in reverse.

Your personal action plan

No matter how much you read about a subject, or how inspired you become, the only way to make any knowledge work for you in a purposeful way is to actually put it into practice.

You have already discovered that by using some of the exercises in this book you have been able to remember nearly 200 things so far. There is nothing like doing something for it to have impact. All too often though, after finishing a course or a book, we put the written material away on a shelf and carry on as before.

That is why preparing a personal action plan is such a good idea. Giving yourself written goals and timelines, putting it somewhere where it will be a constant reminder of what you want to achieve, means you are far more likely to take *and sustain* action.

Select from the following as guidelines, adding more if you need to, then lay out the information to suit you. For example, when considering 'Continue lifelong learning', you might have several topics or areas that you want to tackle under the **How?** heading, with a number of timelines under **When?**

What?	How?	When?
• Become a more positive thinker		
• Adopt a global approach		
• Continue lifelong learning		
• Move out of comfort zones		
• Acknowledge recent successes		
• Obtain optimum health		
• Find time		
• See the advantages		
• Knock down mental barriers		
• Reward yourself		
• Pamper yourself		
• Practise and review		
• Develop your imagination		
• Memorise useful facts		
• Memorise useful numbers		
• Develop new routes for remembering		

Tests

You should now feel confident about your memory, and aware of what you have to do to make it work. The basic principles are simple, and the applications are endless.

Give the information you have to learn

- imagery
- emotional triggers
- exaggeration
- pattern

Anything can be made compatible with the way your memory works, and represented as a set of linked pictures: jobs, names, times, dates, facts, presentations, interview answers, memos, reports. In the right form, your brain can hold unlimited amounts of data.

To confirm the progress you've made since starting this book, take part in this final set of tests. Use any of the techniques you like, individually or in combination. You can make up similar tests yourself in the future to help keep your memory in trim.

Test 1: word list

Memorize the following list of words. Try to do it in less than 5 minutes, then check your success.

sword, handbag, curtain, custard, rake, bomb, trombone, shark, mountain, dragon, leaf, cafe, biscuit, CD, boot, comb, gate, ice, oven, camera

Test 2: job list

Learn this list of jobs. Again, give yourself a maximum of five minutes.

1. order new letterheads
2. take laptop to be repaired
3. arrange meeting with Kelly
4. cancel trip to India
5. go to bank
6. submit invoices
7. play squash
8. call Chris (ext 263)
9. lunch with Andy
10. book holiday, starting August 25th

Test 3: numbers

Use your number system to memorize the following imaginary extension-numbers. You have ten minutes.

Scott: 8305
Rita: 1876
James: 2236
Pam: 4907
Daniel: 9301

Test 4: names

Below is a list of ten people you'll be looking after at a conference. You have ten minutes to learn all their names, so that you can write out the entire list from memory.

Jack Braine, Holly Harper, Christian Attley, Ashley
Verne, Debbie Green, Frank Shepherd, Ray Oates,
Helmut Schreiber, Dougal MacMillan, Hattie Chandler

To finish the test, see how much of the information you've
learned throughout the book is still fresh in your mind.

- the ten items on the shopping list, beginning with
  chocolates
- twenty words on the list, beginning with *television*
- twenty words on the list, beginning with *grass*
- the first ten US Presidents since the Second World War
- the dates of
  - the Gunpowder Plot
  - the death of Ovid
  - the Battle of Waterloo
  - the ruin of Pompeii
  - the birth of Henry VIII
- the dialling-codes for Newcastle, Liverpool, Oxford,
  Peterborough and Birmingham
- the first ten numbers in Japanese
- the ten items to take on holiday
- the ten items on the shopping-list, beginning with *apples*
- the top ten wishes of workers in the research document

Along with the four tests in this chapter, that's 175 distinct
pieces of information – and still just a glimpse of your
memory's infinite power.

Conclusion

Remember:

1. It's important to understand how you learn best.
   What is your preferred learning style? Are you a left- or right-brained thinker?
   Do what you do well, but try to harness the full range of your learning possibilities.
2. You need to organise your learning.
   Look for the easiest ways to arrange the information you have to learn.
   Organise your approach to learning to make the process smooth, quick and fun.
3. You should tap into your imagination.
   Children have a naturally fertile imagination and so can you.
4. Adopt the best mental attitude.
   Be positive. Break bad thinking habits, motivate yourself, reward and encourage yourself.
5. Find the right learning environment.
   What surroundings will encourage you to be at your most receptive?
6. Match your healthy mind with a healthy body.
   Eat well, exercise regularly and get a good night's sleep.
7. You are never too old to learn.
   Don't be tempted to use age as an excuse for not continuing to learn and remember. You have more brain cells than you need, however old you are.

8. Practise.
   Do it! Start using the techniques you have learned in this book, and they will soon become second nature.
9. Be a lifelong learner.
   Keep your brain stimulated and use it to go further in everything you do.
10. Your brain is amazing.
    Never underestimate your learning power. Its potential for storage and creativity is immeasurable.

The average brain has the capacity of an encyclopedia ten billion pages long: start making entries and fill it up.

SUN

MON

TUE

WED

THU

FRI

SAT

For information

on other

IN A **WEEK** titles

go to

www.inaweek.co.uk